Going by Car

by Susan Ashley

Reading consultant: Susan Nations, M.Ed., author/literacy coach/consultant

WEEKLY WR READER®
EARLY LEARNING LIBRARY

Please visit our web site at: www.earlyliteracy.cc
For a free color catalog describing Weekly Reader® Early Learning Library's
list of high-quality books, call 1-877-445-5824 (USA) or 1-800-387-3178 (Canada).
Weekly Reader® Early Learning Library's fax: (414) 336-0164.

Library of Congress Cataloging-in-Publication Data

Ashley, Susan.
    Going by car / by Susan Ashley.
        p. cm. — (Going places)
    Includes bibliographical references and index.
    ISBN 0-8368-3730-4 (lib. bdg.)
    ISBN 0-8368-3835-1 (softcover)
    1. Automobiles—Juvenile literature.   2. Automobile travel—Juvenile literature.
  [1. Automobiles.   2. Automobile travel.]   I. Title.
  TL147.A833   2003
  629.222—dc21   2003045014

This edition first published in 2004 by
Weekly Reader® Early Learning Library
330 West Olive Street, Suite 100
Milwaukee, WI 53212 USA

Art direction: Tammy Gruenewald
Photo research: Diane Laska-Swanke
Editorial assistant: Erin Widenski
Cover and layout design: Katherine A. Goedheer

Photo credits: Cover, title, p. 20 © Gibson Stock Photography; pp. 4, 5, 6, 8, 9, 11, 12, 14, 16,
17, 19, 21 www.ronkimballstock.com; p. 7 Neg. #833.198, From the Collections of Henry Ford
Museum & Greenfield Village; p. 10 Katherine A. Goedheer/© Weekly Reader® Early Learning
Library, 2004; p. 13 © Diane Laska-Swanke; pp. 15, 18 © Gregg Andersen

Printed in the United States of America

1 2 3 4 5 6 7 8 9 07 06 05 04 03

Table of Contents

The first cars were called "horseless carriages."
Can you guess why?

Cars of the Past

Can you imagine a time when there were
no cars? Before the car was invented,
people used horse-drawn vehicles for
transportation. In fact, the first cars were
called horseless carriages.

Early cars did not have roofs or windows. Most roads were dirt roads. Drivers wore long coats and hats to keep warm and clean. They wore goggles to protect their eyes from the dust on the road.

People often got dirty when they rode in open cars like this one.

The Model T was one of the most popular
cars ever made.

The first cars were too expensive for most
people. In 1908, Henry Ford decided to
build a car that everyone could afford —
the Model T. Using standard parts and a
moving assembly line, Ford's factories could
build Model Ts quickly and cheaply.

The Ford assembly line used teams of workers to build each car. As a car moved along the line, a different team would add a new part until the car was finished. Today, assembly lines are still used to build cars.

These two men are working on a Ford assembly line in 1913.

This 1937 Cadillac La Salle has a long,
sleek body and plenty of curves.

Model Ts were short cars with sharp,
straight lines. By the 1930s, cars had
become longer, with smooth, round lines.
Car designs continued to change. In the
1950s, cars were known for their fancy
grills in front and their tailfins in back.

The 1950s were also famous for drive-ins. People ate in their cars at drive-in restaurants. They watched movies in their cars at drive-in theaters. Today, there are drive-thru banks, drive-thru car washes, and drive-thru restaurants.

This red 1932 Ford and yellow 1957 Chevy show off their bright colors in front of a diner.

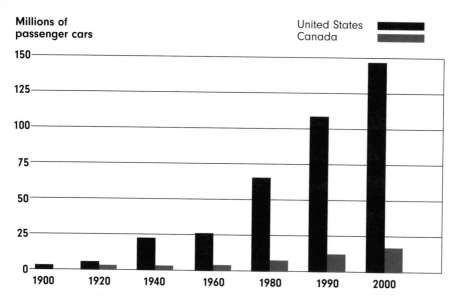

Millions of passenger cars

United States ■
Canada ■

This graph shows how many cars people owned in the United States and Canada between 1900 and 2000.

Cars Today

There are millions of cars on the road today. They come in many styles and sizes. One of the most common styles is the sedan. A sedan has four doors and front and back seats.

Sports cars are small and often have room for only two people. They are fast and built low to the ground. Many sports cars are convertibles. Convertibles are cars with tops that fold down for driving in nice weather.

This sports car convertible has its top down.

**Station wagons are long cars
with lots of room.**

Station wagons and minivans are popular
with families. They are big cars that can
hold more people than a sedan. They
have lots of room for groceries and
luggage.

Sport utility vehicles (S.U.V.s) are large cars that can handle city streets or rugged roads. They are built high off the ground and have four-wheel drive. This allows them to ride through mud and snow without getting stuck.

Sport utility vehicles are easy to handle in the snow.

This **PT Cruiser** looks like cars from the past.

Today, some new cars actually look like cars from the past. Cars like the PT Cruiser and the New Beetle are based on designs that were popular many years ago.

Safety is very important in cars today. Seat belts and air bags can help prevent injury in an accident. New car designs are tested in many ways to make sure the cars are as safe as possible.

Seat belts and car seats are important safety features in any car.

**Dragsters have long, narrow bodies.
This one is roaring down the track!**

Special Cars

Some cars are designed for special
purposes. Race cars are built to go very
fast. There are many types of race cars.
Indy Cars have wide wheels to grip the
track at high speeds. Dragsters race on
a long, straight track called a drag strip.

A police car is not like other cars. It has flashing lights on its roof. The word "POLICE" is painted on the outside of the car. A computer and two-way radios inside the car help the police do their job. A police car has something else most cars do not have: a siren!

The lights on top of this police car flash on and off.

Taxis are often painted bright colors so people can easily see them.

A taxi is a car that people hire for short trips. Taxis are common in big cities and at airports. Passengers pay a taxi driver money, called a fare, to ride the taxi. The fare is based on how far they are going and how much time it takes to get there.

A limousine is a large, comfortable car hired for special occasions. Stretch limousines are the longest cars of all. They look like cars that have been s-t-r-e-t-c-h-e-d as far as they can go!

The Lincoln Town Car is a popular stretch limousine. A car this long can hold many people!

Cars that use gasoline for
fuel create air pollution.

Cars of the Future

Most cars today use gasoline for fuel. Gas
is expensive and causes air pollution. Cars
of the future may use electricity for fuel.
Electric cars are quiet and create less
pollution.

Electric cars are designed to save power in many ways. Some use batteries. Others get their power from the Sun.

Car designs are changing all the time. Would you like to design a car someday?

This General Motors EV1 car is powered by electricity.

Glossary

air bag — a bag that inflates on impact to protect passengers in a car accident

carriage — a horse-drawn vehicle used to carry people

fare — the price a person pays to travel

goggles — eyeglasses worn to protect the eyes from dust, wind, and flying objects

occasion — an important or special event

vehicle — something used to transport people or goods

For More Information

Books
Flammang, James M. *Cars*. Berkeley Heights: Enslow
   Publishers, 2001.
Raby, Philip. *Racing Cars*. Minneapolis: Lerner
   Publications Company, 1999.
Sutton, Richard. *Car*. New York: DK Publishing, 2000.
Wright, David. *Classic Cars* (series). Milwaukee: Gareth
   Stevens, Inc., 2002.

Web Sites
Autos
channels.netscape.com/ns/autos/photo.jsp
Photo gallery of new cars and concept cars from the
2003 Detroit Auto Show

Built for Speed
www.pbs.org/wgbh/amex/kids/tech1900/car.html
A history of early automobiles

Model T Road Trip
www.hfmgv.org/education/smartfun/welcome.html
Join a fictional family on a road trip across America

Index